Tortuga Squad

Kids Saving Sea Turtles in Costa Rica

Cathleen Burnham

CRICKHOLLOW BOOKS

Crickhollow Books is an imprint of Great Lakes Literary, based in Milwaukee, Wisconsin, an independent press publishing quality fiction and nonfiction.

Our titles are available from your favorite bookstore or from trade wholesalers or library jobbers. For a complete catalog of all our titles or to place educational bulk orders, visit our website:

www.CrickhollowBooks.com

For a teacher's guide & more content resources for this WAKA series (World Association of Kids & Animals), which includes *Doyli to the Rescue, Tortuga Squad,* and other books about kids around the world involved in grassroots projects to protect endangered wild animals and their habitats, visit:

www.WAKABooks.org

Tortuga Squad: Kids Saving Sea Turtles in Costa Rica
© 2016, Cathleen Burnham

Photos by Cathleen Burnham, with additional photography by Kenyon Burnham and Bay Burnham. Loggerhead turtle photo on pp. 14–15 is courtesy NOAA (National Oceanic and Atmospheric Administration). Book design by Melissa Thoroughgood. Cover design by Meilssa Thoroughgood and Philip Martin.

ISBN: 978-1-933987-24-8

Note: this replaces an earlier softcover edition, ISBN 978-0-9836666-4-6, published by the author in 2011.

Summary: *Tortuga Squad: Kids Saving Sea Turtles in Costa Rica,* by photodocumentary journalist Cathleen Burnham, (Book 2 in the WAKA book series) introduces us to a group of kids who live on an island in Costa Rica and work to save baby turtles, patrolling the beach for poachers and rescuing eggs to incubate in a protected hatchery.

BISAC Codes
JNF003220 JUVENILE NONFICTION / Animals / Animal Welfare
JNF003190 JUVENILE NONFICTION / Animals / Reptiles & Amphibians (Sea Turtles)
JNF003270 JUVENILE NONFICTION / Animals / Endangered
JNF038050 JUVENILE NONFICTION / People & Places / Caribbean & Latin America
JNF037020 JUVENILE NONFICTION / Science & Nature / Environmental Conservation & Protection

TOPICS: Caribbean Sea, Costa Rica, global kids, youth activism, wild animal rescue & conservation.

First Crickhollow Books Edition
Printed in Canada

Tortuga Squad

Kids Saving Sea Turtles in Costa Rica

Cathleen Burnham

CRICKHOLLOW BOOKS

Central America

Costa Rica

MEXICO

HONDURAS

EL SALVADOR

NICARAGUA

Caribbean Sea

COSTA RICA

Parismina●

★ San José

Pacific Ocean

PANAMA

2

NICARAGUA

Legend

—— River

COSTA RICA

Parismina

San José

PANAMA

3

The mother turtle swam through the surf and then dragged herself onto the black sand beach of Parismina Island, in Costa Rica. She lumbered across the sand. She stopped where the palm trees and tall dune grasses begin to grow. With her hind flippers, she dug a deep hole. Into the hole she dropped leathery, white eggs — over 80 of them!

But, before she could cover her precious eggs back up with sand and return to the sea, a man emerged from the bushes. He ran to her, and with one giant heave, flipped the mother turtle onto her back. She was helpless.

Quickly, the man filled a plastic bag with every one of her eggs. Then he dragged the mother sea turtle into the brush. Later, he would return and make her his supper.

People on Parismina have always eaten turtle meat and eggs. But many sea turtles have become close to extinction. Poaching eggs or killing sea turtles is now illegal. Some people still do it, though.

Once the man was sure the turtle was well hidden, he snuck back to his village as the sun began to rise. Upside-down, the mama sea turtle's legs waved desperately in the air. Moments later, a little girl's head popped up out of the bushes.

Her name is Bianca, and she is just six years old. She scanned the shore, afraid the man might return.

When she was sure the coast was clear, she ran to the spot she'd seen the man leave the turtle. Bianca parted the branches and leaned in.

"Hold on, mama turtle. You're too big for me, but I'll be back." The turtle's black, shining eyes stared up at Bianca.

Bianca raced down the dirt road and knocked on her friend Christian's door. Bianca, Christian, and all the kids of Parismina were part of the Tortuga Squad. "Tortuga" means "turtle" in Spanish, and Tortuga Squad is the name the kids gave themselves because they help save turtles.

"Help! Poacher! A mama green turtle is trapped on her back!" Bianca whispered through the door.

Sleepy children came outside. Other village children who had heard Bianca soon joined them.

"Where?" ten-year-old Christian asked.

"Follow me," said Bianca, and she led them to the stranded green turtle.

"It won't be easy. This mama weighs hundreds of pounds," said Dylan. But they all pitched in and gave a mighty push. They flipped the turtle back over and watched her escape into the waves.

"Did you see the poacher?" asked a girl named Melany.

Bianca nodded. "I sure did. It was Señor Carlos," she said. "He took all the eggs!"

Everyone groaned. The Tortuga Squad worked hard to protect turtles and their eggs from poachers. They had even built a hatchery to safeguard the eggs until they hatched.

This time of year, late May, many turtles laid eggs, and baby turtles were hatching daily. These kids were busy.

The young members of the Tortuga Squad patrolled the beach every evening to keep poachers at bay. Adults and teenagers then guarded the beach all night. But Carlos, the poacher, had slipped down to the beach after the last patrol. This unlucky green sea turtle had come ashore early in the morning to lay her eggs, rather than at night when patrollers had been watching.

Melany set off at a run to Carlos' house, but when she got there he was gone. She came back to the other children. "He's gone," she reported. "He's left to take the eggs to market."

Turtle eggs at market.

"At least we saved the mother," said Diana.

"Yes. He'll get a surprise when he comes back for her tonight," said Ariel.

Realizing that there was nothing more they could do, the kids walked home along their village's dirt paths. They arrived at their homes just in time for breakfast.

Leatherbacks are Endangered

At breakfast, Melany told her mother about what had happened to the green sea turtle. "You were brave to go back to the beach and save the turtle," Melany's mother replied. Just then, her father came home from his job. Before dawn each morning, her dad took tourists deep-sea fishing.

"I just caught the end of your conversation. What happened?" asked her father as he sat down at the kitchen table.

"The kids flipped a poached turtle back over. They saved it! The poacher was Carlos. Unfortunately, he got all the eggs," said her mother.

Melany's father sighed, then ladled rice and beans onto his plate. "This morning, a leatherback was caught in some nets that a commercial fisherman hauled up. I could see it on the deck of their boat. The poor thing had drowned in the nets." He shook his head.

Depths that Turtles can Swim

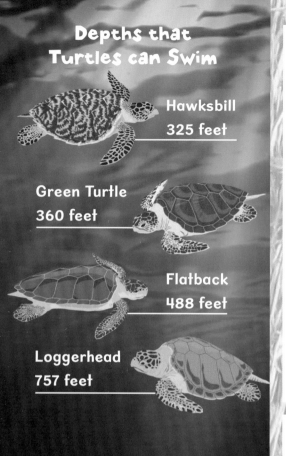

Hawksbill
325 feet

Green Turtle
360 feet

Flatback
488 feet

Loggerhead
757 feet

Leatherback
3900 feet

"Leatherbacks are endangered!" cried Melany. "We can't let them die. They've been around since the time of the dinosaurs."

"I know. Those commercial fishermen could use nets with a built-in escape route for turtles," said her father. "But they don't want to spend the money for new nets. If they don't start using the right nets soon, leatherback turtles will be extinct in a few years."

Above: A loggerhead turtle escapes a fishing net equipped with a Turtle Excluder Device (TED). Photo: NOAA

Above Left: Many sea turtles become tangled in commercial fishing nets and drown.

Below Left: New commercial fishing nets have Turtle Excluder Devices that allow turtles to escape.

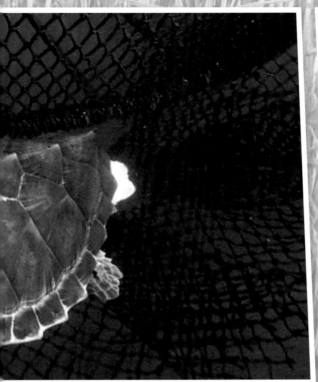

The family finished their breakfast in silence. As Melany wiped the last dish clean, her mother took money from a jar hidden behind a bag of rice.

"Melany, we need bananas, coffee, and mangos from the market today," she said.

Melany loved going to the mainland to the busy town of Siquirres. The market town had modern buildings, cars, and crowds of people, not to mention all the wonderful things to buy — pretty clothes, movies on DVD, and delicious food. Even if they didn't have money to buy the fancy goods, it was still fun to browse.

15

Saving Another Endangered Animal at Sea

Melany and her mother left for the island dock. They paid a boat driver a few coins and settled into their seats for the 15-minute ride. Just beneath the surface of the water, they saw a caiman lurking. A pelican stood on shore with a large fish in its mouth. As she looked around, Melany saw a sloth, crocodiles, and many beautiful birds.

sloth

pelican

caimans

Melany stared dreamily out into the water, watching a coconut bob in the surf. But then the "coconut" turned a little, and Melany saw two eyes staring out from it.

She rose from her seat and shouted, "That's not a coconut!"

Her mother looked embarrassed at her daughter's behavior but wondered what she meant.

"What's not a coconut, honey?" asked Melany's mother.

Melany pointed down at the surf. The boat driver and her mother looked out at the little head bobbing in the water.

"I . . . I think it's a monkey." The driver squinted and slowed down.

"We have to save it!" cried Melany.

"If we bring that thing aboard, it could bite us," said the driver.

"We can't leave it to drown," scolded Melany's mother.

"It's a howler monkey. They're endangered," pleaded Melany. The man growled, but he turned his boat toward the little head. When he came close, he stretched an oar out. The monkey grasped it. The driver slowly pulled the oar to the boat.

As soon as the monkey was close enough to the boat, the driver grabbed it by the scruff of its neck. Then he hauled the little monkey onto the side of the boat.

The exhausted howler clung there for dear life. The driver steered his vessel toward shore. Melany and her mother barely breathed, afraid they might frighten the monkey. Then he could fall back into the water.

But they needn't have worried. When the boat neared shore, the howler jumped off the boat into the shallow water and began the trip back into the jungle. Soon they saw him peering out from the high branches of a tree.

The boat driver beamed. "Hey! The little fellow made it!"

Melany's mother told the driver, "You can tell your family you saved an endangered animal! Your children and wife will be proud of you."

"That was a brave thing you did," said Melany. "You could have been bitten."

"It was nothing," said the driver, but Melany could tell he was proud.

Soon they reached the port of Caño Blanco. Melany and her mother boarded a bus for the two-hour ride to Siquirres. They drove through banana groves that had once been a great jungle — a beautiful rainforest home to jaguars, sloths, and monkeys. Now, there were only bananas — and more bananas.

Finding Turtle Eggs Where They Don't Belong

At Siquirres Market, Melany looked at the stalls filled with fruits and vegetables. Suddenly she heard a man calling, "Huevos Tortugas! Huevos Tortugas!" Turtle eggs!

She turned, and there was Carlos from Parismina Island selling eggs — the eggs from that morning. They were stored in a cooler he'd rigged to a bicycle. She felt sick as she saw a man stop to purchase the eggs. Every one of those eggs should have grown into a precious baby turtle meant to swim the seas.

Carlos knew selling turtle eggs was illegal — everyone did. But he still did it. Melany looked around for a policeman, but didn't see one. She glared at Carlos, even though he didn't see her. He disappeared around a corner, and Melany knew there was nothing more to be done.

Melany and her mom made their purchases and returned home.

Back on Parismina Island, Melany looked for her friends. She was dying to tell them about the howler monkey rescue — and how she'd seen Carlos selling eggs in the market. But Christian, Whitney, Diana, little Bianca, and the rest of the squad were nowhere to be found in the village. So she walked to the beach.

The Tortuga Squad has convinced former poachers to help. This old man was one of the island's worst poachers. But, every day, his grandchildren told him stories about protecting turtles. When he saw how hard his grandchildren worked, he stopped poaching completely. Now he is the Turtle Hatchery Guard.

24

When Melany arrived, she promptly forgot all about her news. Jezebel, a well-loved dog, was causing trouble. She was digging up a turtle nest! Dogs can sniff turtle eggs under the sand. They dig them up and eat them.

Melany's friends were already there, trying to stop Jezebel. It was their job to protect baby turtles. After all, if they didn't, who would?

All of the kids chased Jezebel away from the beach. Keeping turtle nests safe was a busy job for the Tortuga Squad.

The next morning, all the kids were at the village community center, dancing to music blaring from a boom box

Suddenly, Christian came to the door out of breath. "Leatherback babies. Hatchlings!" was all he said before disappearing from the doorway.

All the kids knew what he meant. They raced out of the community center and headed straight for the beach. Peering over the fence of the turtle hatchery, the children saw that a nest of tiny leatherback turtles had hatched.

Ariel and her father scooped the baby turtles into a bucket. They carried the bucket out of the hatchery to the beach.

There, they gently placed the bucket on its side. The baby leatherbacks crawled out of the bucket and made their way toward the surf.

The Journey to the Ocean

The trip across the beach was perilous for the baby turtles. Birds tried to scoop them up in their beaks. The kids waved their arms to scare the birds away. Dogs hoped to snap up a tasty treat, but the Squad ran them off. Crabs caught babies in their pinchers and dragged them toward their lairs. The kids pulled the babies out of pinchers and set them back on course for the sea.

The temperature of the sand determines whether leatherback turtle babies will be male or female.

As they worked, the kids were careful not to create footprints in the baby turtles' paths. They knew a turtle could easily tumble into a footprint and become trapped. When the waves crashed in, they washed lots of sand into the footprint. If the turtle was still there, he might be buried.

The little turtles used their flippers to race to the ocean. The children worked hard to make sure every turtle made it — and every turtle did.

After watching all the baby turtles make it safely into the water, Melany, Bianca, and the other children of the Tortuga Squad sat on the beach. They watched quietly as little turtle heads popped in and out of the water. The little tortugas were swimming hard. They needed to make it over the shallow reef and to the ocean floor.

There, they would hide among sea plants, resting for two days before swimming farther out to the open ocean.

Once they were at sea, the kids could no longer protect the baby turtles from hungry fish, but at least they had saved them from the dangers of land: crabs, dogs, birds . . . and poachers. It was all in a day's work for the Tortuga Squad.

To learn more about the Tortuga Squad and other stories of kids doing amazing things to protect wild animals around the globe, visit:

WAKABooks.org

What's Next?

A NOTE FROM THE AUTHOR

Located on the Caribbean coast of Costa Rica, Parismina is an isolated island. There is no bridge to the mainland, and no paved roads on the island. The families of Parismina are very poor. For generations, these islanders have eaten turtle meat as a part of their diet.

But now, with the encouragement of conservationists, most villagers have come together to take a stand against hunting endangered sea turtles and poaching their eggs.

The island is visited by leatherbacks, green turtles, and hawksbill turtles. They swim in the sea, and the mothers come ashore to lay their eggs. But it's a dangerous place for the turtles. Although stealing the eggs or killing sea turtles for meat is now illegal, some people still do it. And there are natural predators.

When they are ready to lay eggs, adult female sea turtles crawl up onto land to make a nest. The mother turtle hauls herself onto a sandy beach, nearly always at night. Using her hind flippers, she digs a hole 16 to 20 inches deep. The female then starts filling the nest with soft-shelled eggs, one by one, until she has deposited around 50 to 200 eggs, depending on the species.

After laying, she refills the hole with sand, smoothing the surface to hide the nest. She then returns to the ocean.

After about two months, the eggs hatch. The hatchlings tear their shells apart with their snouts and dig up through the sand. The babies turtles emerge and instinctively head towards the sea.

But there are many dangers. Dogs will dig for eggs before they hatch. Birds or crabs will try to eat the small turtles. But the greatest danger is from humans – poachers who may try to capture a mother turtle for the meat or gather the eggs to sell in dark corners of markets on the mainland.

On Parismina, concerned individuals and organizations working to save sea turtles often invite volunteers to visit the island and help in preservation efforts, as my family did.

But best of all, the locals see the need to get involved. I was most impressed and delighted to meet the island kids who were doing their part to save the turtles. So we came together to make this story of the Tortuga Squad activities.

Tortuga means *turtle* in Spanish. Tortuga Squad is the name the kids gave themselves. They patrol the beach during hatching season, and they helped build a hatchery – a fenced-in enclosure where they can protect eggs until they hatch.

These stories shine a light on models of small-scale activism: young people who are kind, caring, and involved. We've all seen animals suffer, whether in person or via media. It's painful for us all. And we may think, "There's nothing I can do."

You can do something. You can get involved, too.

❖　❖　❖

This story is a seed. Maybe you and your friends or classmates can come up with something you can do, in a small way, to help protect other creatures who might need a helping hand.

For more ideas and stories of what others are doing around the world, visit:

www.WAKABooks.org

WAKA stands for World Association of Kids and Animals. It's a way to share stories of real kids – young people not so different from you and your friends – who found a way to get involved and help protect wild animals.

– Cathleen Burnham